What's Inside This Book

1. Five Chapters of Incredible Facts
Dive into five exciting chapters filled with mind-blowing, weird, and wonderful facts about animals, space, food, history, and the human body. Each fact is designed to surprise and entertain you!

2. Guess the Fact" Section
Test your knowledge and have fun with 10 tricky guesses! Can you figure out which statement is true? Challenge your friends and see who knows more!

3. Maze Madness
End your journey with 5 exciting mazes to solve. These puzzles are a fun way to keep your brain sharp and entertained! Get ready to explore, guess, and solve!

Incredible
but
True!

chapters:

- Animals: Unbelievable traits and behaviors.

- Space: Mind-blowing facts about planets and stars.

- Human Body: Odd things about our own biology.

- History: Bizarre events or ancient practices.

- Food: Strange but true facts about what we eat.

Animals

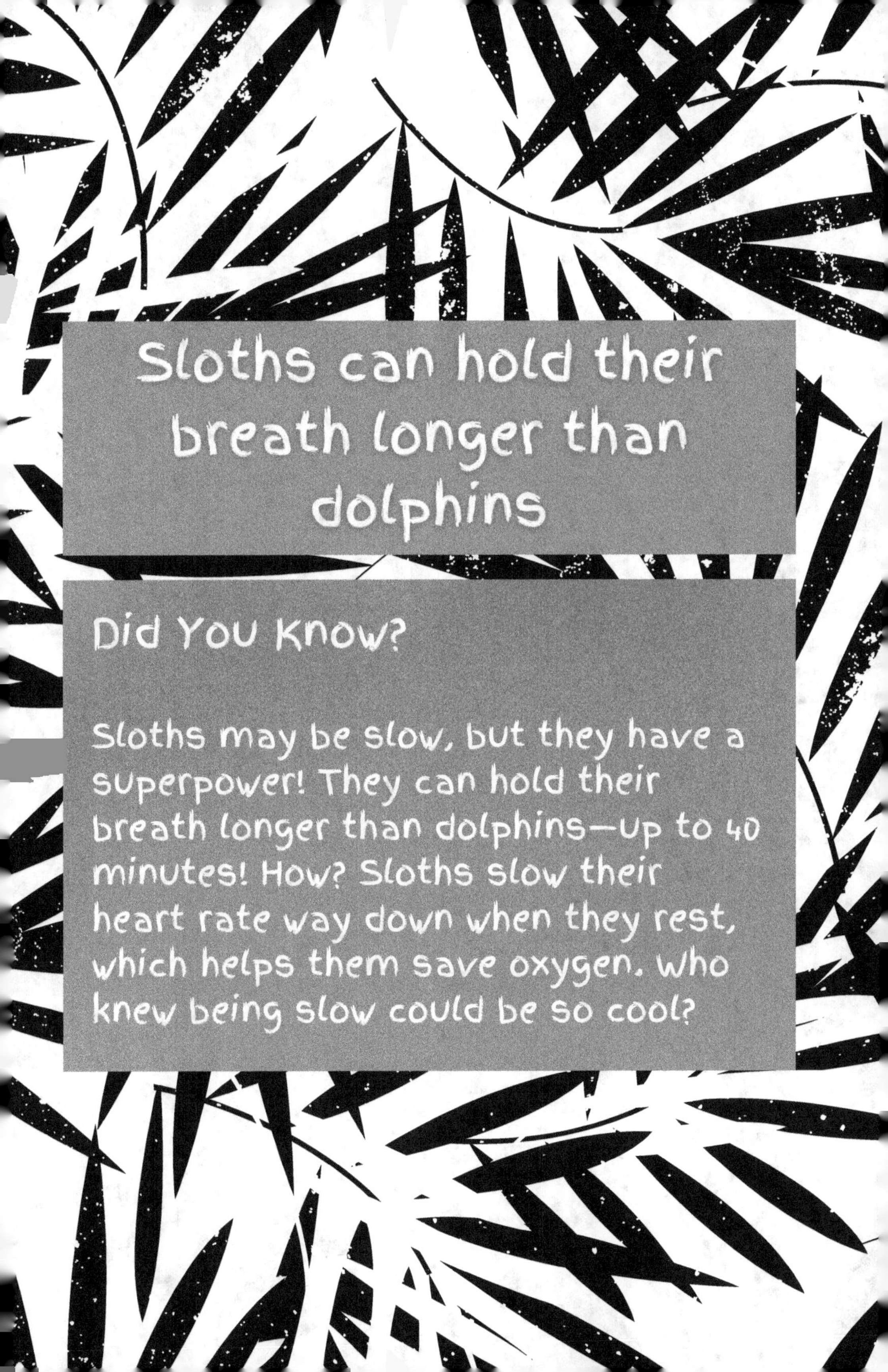

Sloths can hold their breath longer than dolphins

Did You Know?

Sloths may be slow, but they have a superpower! They can hold their breath longer than dolphins—up to 40 minutes! How? Sloths slow their heart rate way down when they rest, which helps them save oxygen. Who knew being slow could be so cool?

Octopuses have three hearts and blue blood.

Did You Know?

Octopuses are amazing creatures with not one, not two, but THREE hearts! Two hearts pump blood to their gills, while the third heart sends it to the rest of their body. But that's not all—octopus blood is blue, not red like ours! This is because their blood has a special chemical called hemocyanin, which helps them survive in deep, cold waters.
Oh, and here's something cool: when an octopus is swimming, the heart that pumps blood to its body actually stops beating! These clever creatures are full of surprises, don't you think?

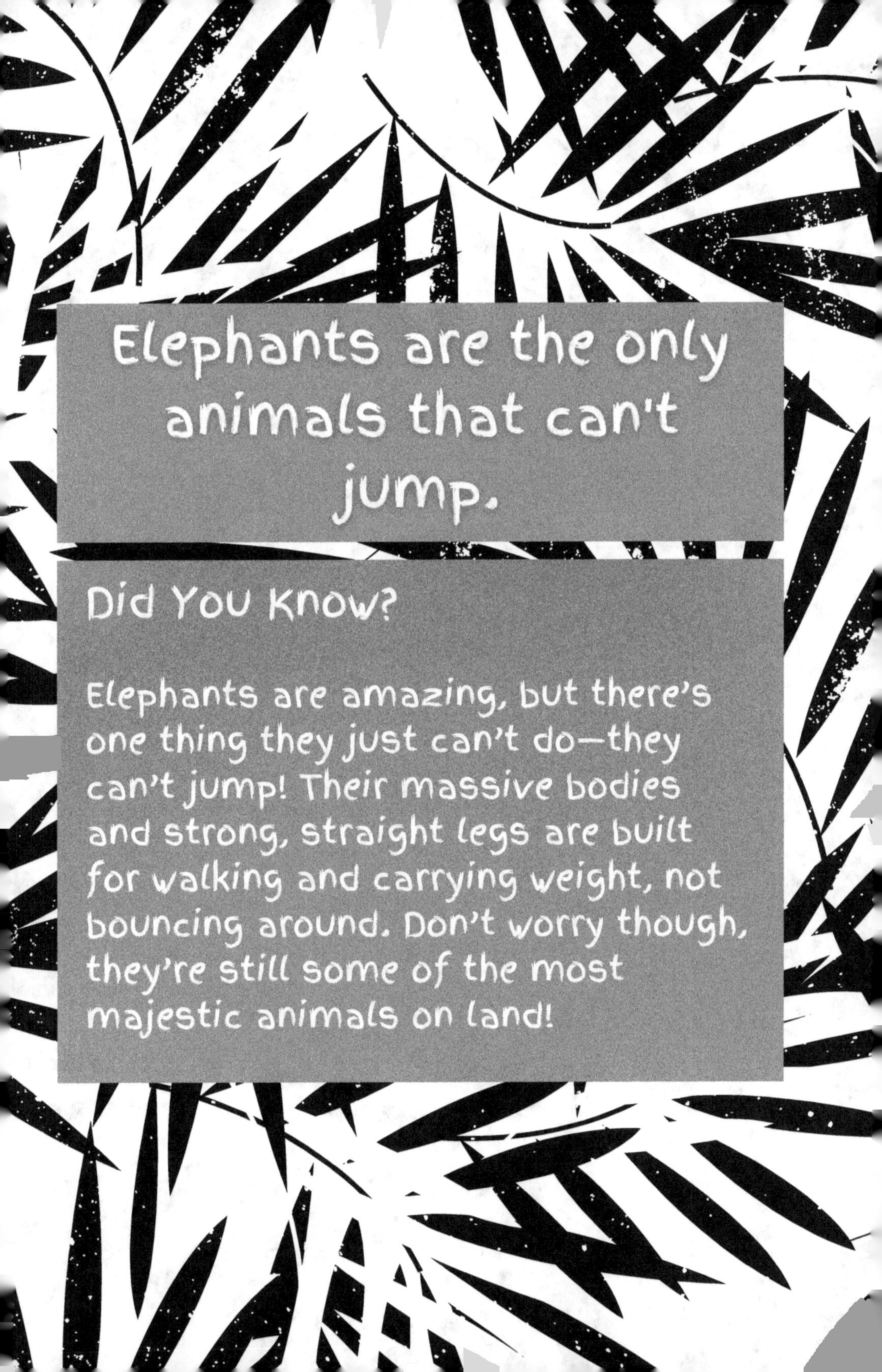

Elephants are the only animals that can't jump.

Did You Know?

Elephants are amazing, but there's one thing they just can't do—they can't jump! Their massive bodies and strong, straight legs are built for walking and carrying weight, not bouncing around. Don't worry though, they're still some of the most majestic animals on land!

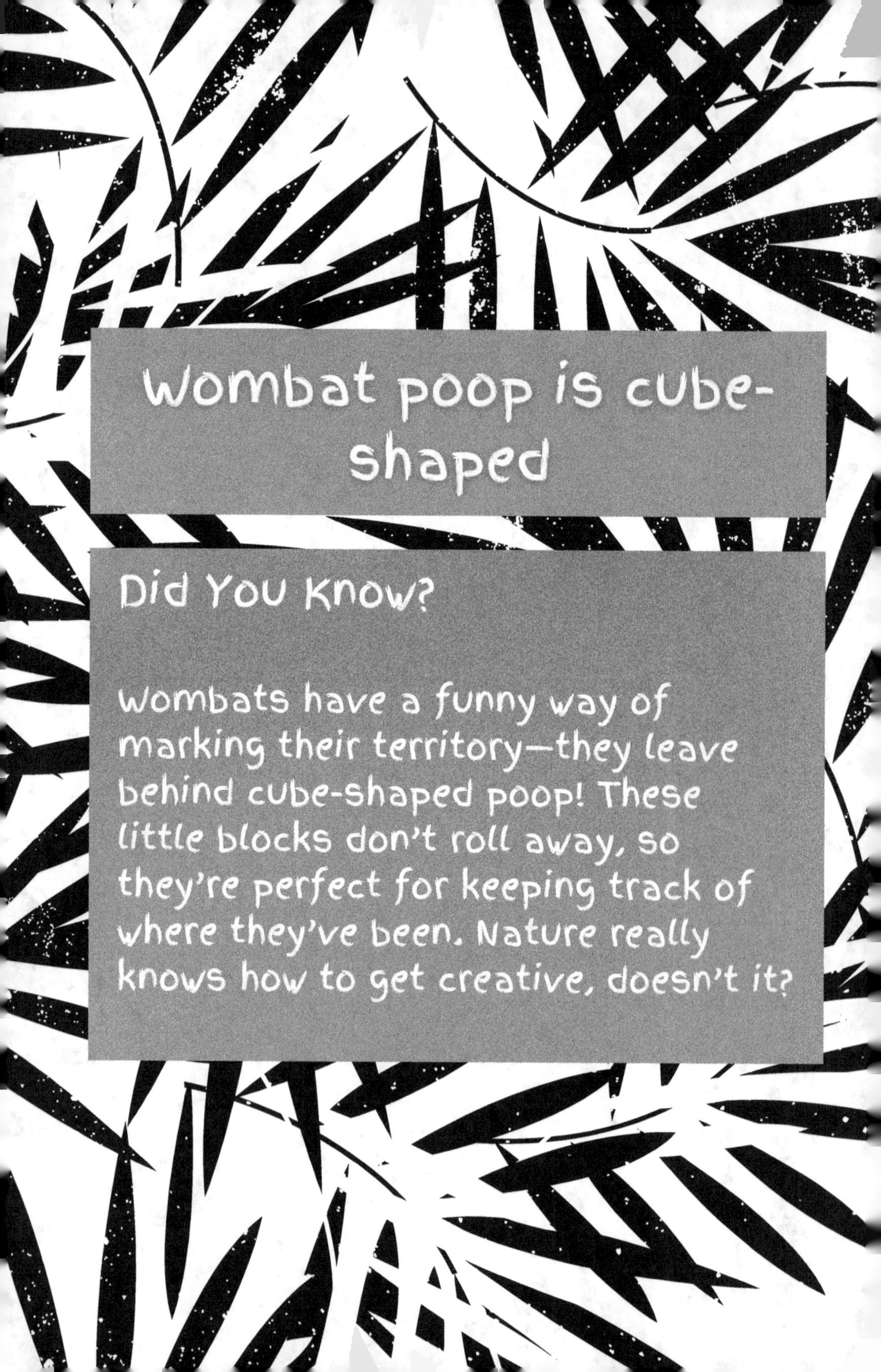

Wombat poop is cube-shaped

Did You Know?

Wombats have a funny way of marking their territory—they leave behind cube-shaped poop! These little blocks don't roll away, so they're perfect for keeping track of where they've been. Nature really knows how to get creative, doesn't it?

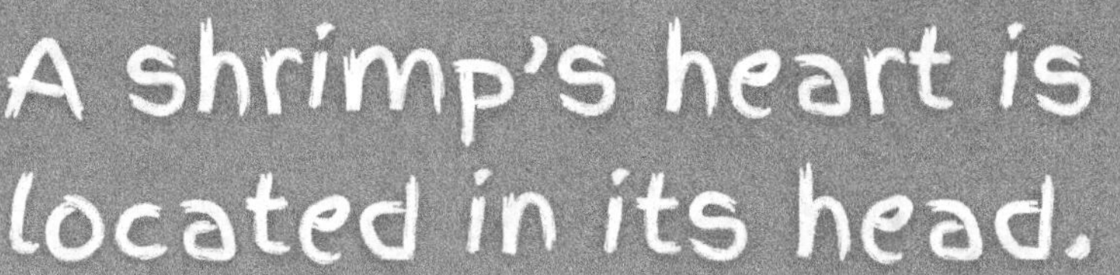

A shrimp's heart is located in its head.

Did You Know?

Shrimp have their hearts in the most unexpected place—in their heads! But wait, it's not as strange as it sounds. A shrimp's head and chest are covered by a hard shell called the cephalothorax, and that's where its tiny heart is located.
Shrimp might be small, but they're super cool. Their bodies are designed perfectly for swimming and snapping up food. Isn't it amazing how animals can have such different and surprising designs?

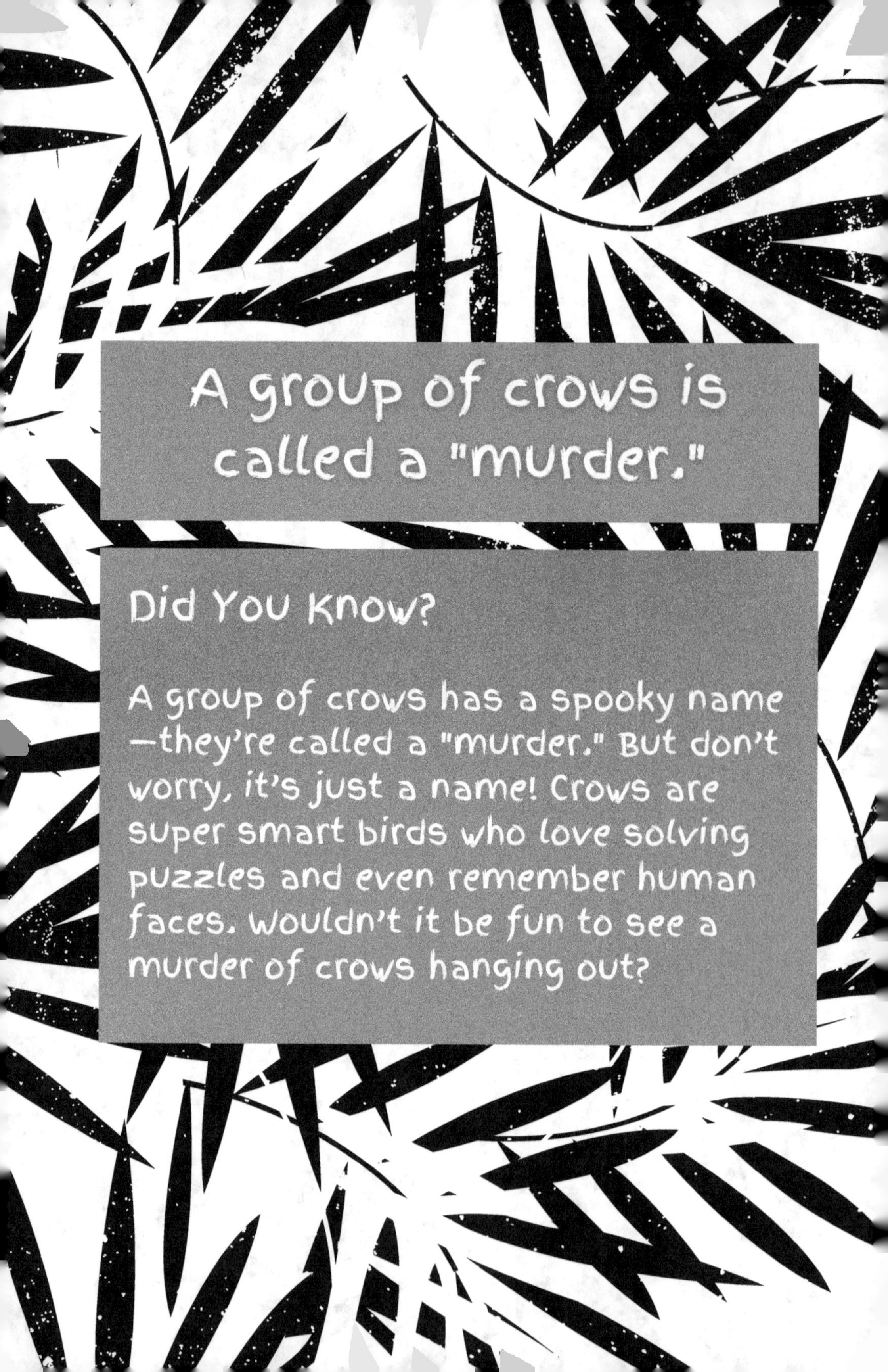

A group of crows is
called a "murder."

Did You Know?

A group of crows has a spooky name
—they're called a "murder." But don't
worry, it's just a name! Crows are
super smart birds who love solving
puzzles and even remember human
faces. Wouldn't it be fun to see a
murder of crows hanging out?

Sea otters hold hands while sleeping

Did You Know?

Sea otters are the cutest snugglers of the sea! They hold hands while sleeping to keep from drifting apart in the water. This is called a "raft," and it helps them stay close and safe. Who wouldn't love a hand-holding buddy like that?

Frogs can freeze solid in winter and thaw out alive in spring.

Did You Know?

Some frogs are like nature's little ice cubes! They can freeze solid in the winter, stopping their heartbeat and breathing. But when spring comes, they thaw out and hop back to life. Talk about a frosty superpower!

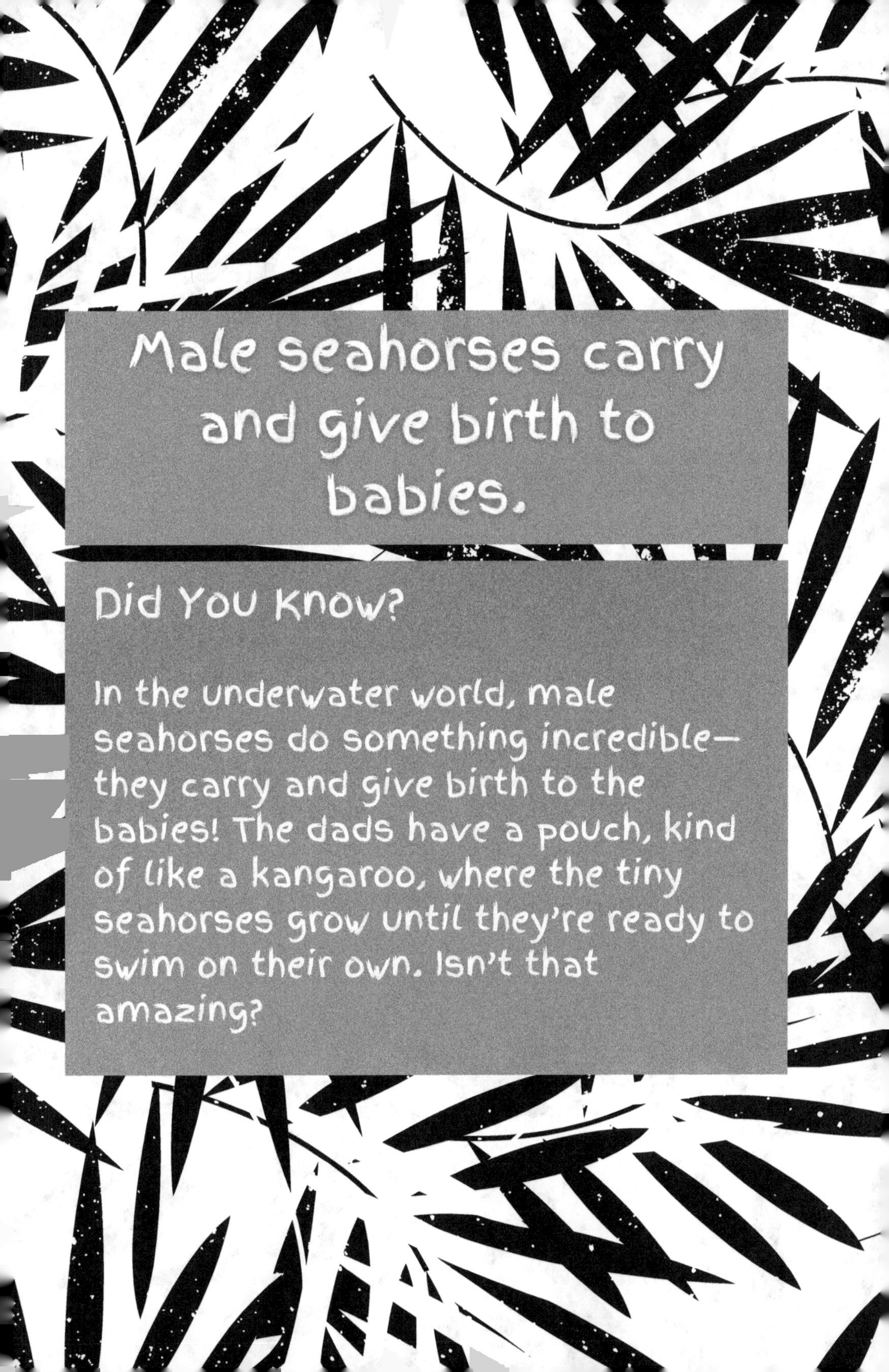

Male seahorses carry and give birth to babies.

Did You Know?

In the underwater world, male seahorses do something incredible—they carry and give birth to the babies! The dads have a pouch, kind of like a kangaroo, where the tiny seahorses grow until they're ready to swim on their own. Isn't that amazing?

Kangaroos can't walk backward.

Did You Know?

Kangaroos are famous for hopping, but did you know they can't walk backward? Their long tails and powerful legs make it impossible. That's okay—they're built for bounding forward into the outback instead!

space

A day on Venus is longer than a year on Venus.

Did You Know?

Venus is a strange planet. A single day on Venus—how long it takes to spin once—lasts longer than a whole year there! That's because it spins super slowly while zooming around the Sun. Imagine celebrating your birthday every "day"!

There's a planet made of diamonds called "55 Cancri e."

Did You Know?

Out in space, there's a planet called 55 Cancri e that's made of diamonds! This sparkling world is so far away that we can only imagine how shiny it must be. It's like a giant treasure floating in the galaxy!

The Sun's core is 27 million degrees

Did You Know?

The Sun is so powerful because its core reaches an unbelievable temperature—27 million degrees Fahrenheit! That's so hot it could melt anything in seconds. Good thing we're far enough away to enjoy its warmth safely!

On the moon, your footprints can last millions of years

Did You Know?

If you walked on the Moon, your footprints would stay there for millions of years! That's because the Moon has no wind or rain to wash them away. It's like leaving your mark on a giant, dusty time capsule.

Space smells like burnt steak, according to astronauts.

Did You Know?

Astronauts say space has a strange smell—like burnt steak! Even though you can't smell space directly, their spacesuits pick up the scent during spacewalks. Who knew outer space had a smoky aroma?

Saturn's moon, Titan, has rivers and lakes of liquid methane.

Did You Know?

Saturn's moon, Titan, has rivers and lakes, but they're not made of water—they're full of liquid methane! Methane is so cold and weird that it can flow like water on this chilly moon. It's like a frozen alien world!

If you could fold a piece of paper 42 times, it would be thick enough to reach the Moon.

Did You Know?

If you could fold a piece of paper 42 times, it would be tall enough to reach the Moon! Each fold doubles the thickness, so it grows super fast. Try folding one and see how far you get! (Hint: it gets hard around seven folds.)

Neutron stars are so dense that a sugar-cube-sized amount of their material would weigh a billion tons.

Did You Know?

Neutron stars are tiny but unbelievably dense. Just a sugar-cube-sized piece of one would weigh a billion tons! That's heavier than all the cars on Earth combined. These stars are small but mighty!

Venus spins backward compared to most planets.

Did You Know?

Most planets spin the same way, but Venus decided to be different—it spins backward! If you lived there, the Sun would rise in the west and set in the east. Talk about a topsy-turvy world!

Jupiter has a storm, the Great Red Spot, that's been raging for over 300 years.

Did You Know?

Jupiter has a giant storm called the Great Red Spot that's been raging for over 300 years! It's so big that Earth could fit inside it. Imagine a hurricane that never ends—it's a weather wonder!

Human-Body

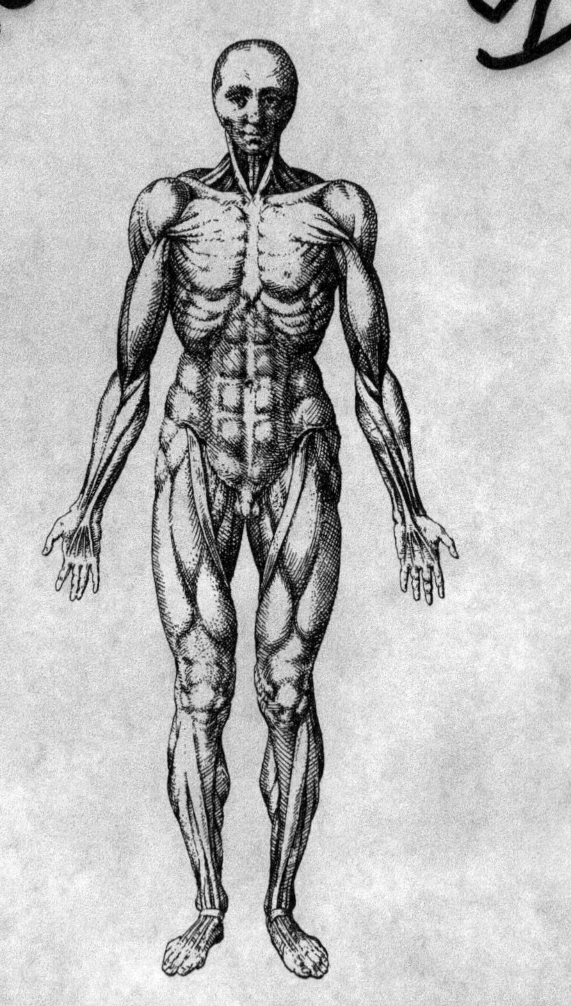

Your stomach gets a new lining every three days to prevent it from digesting itself.

Did You Know?

Your stomach gets a brand-new lining every three days. Why? To protect itself from the super-strong acids it uses to digest food. Without this refresh, your stomach might start digesting itself!

You produce about 25,000 quarts of saliva in a lifetime

Did You Know?

In your lifetime, you produce about 25,000 quarts of saliva—that's enough to fill two swimming pools! Saliva helps you chew, swallow, and even fight germs. Who knew spit was so useful?

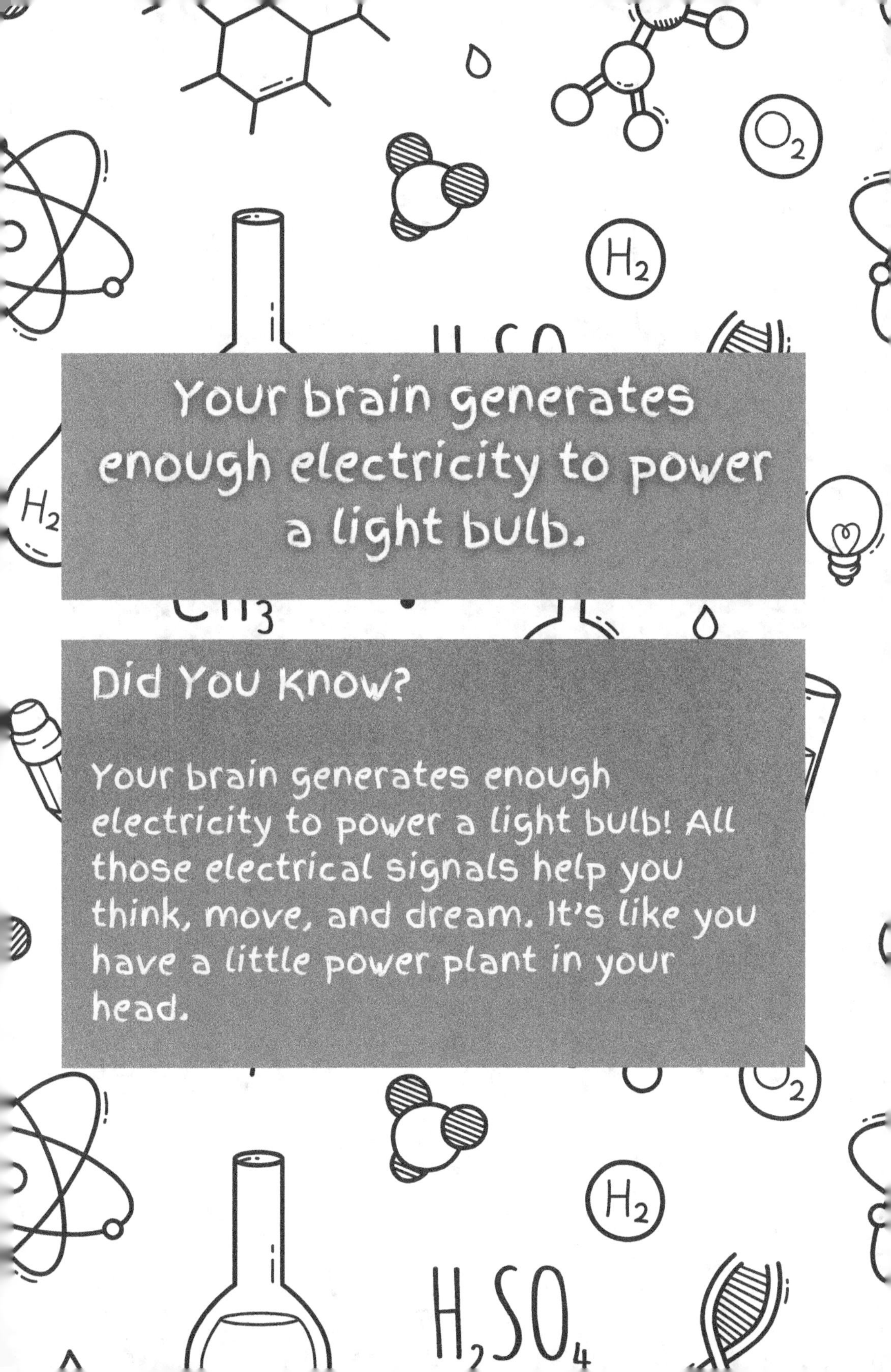

Your brain generates enough electricity to power a light bulb.

Did You Know?

Your brain generates enough electricity to power a light bulb! All those electrical signals help you think, move, and dream. It's like you have a little power plant in your head.

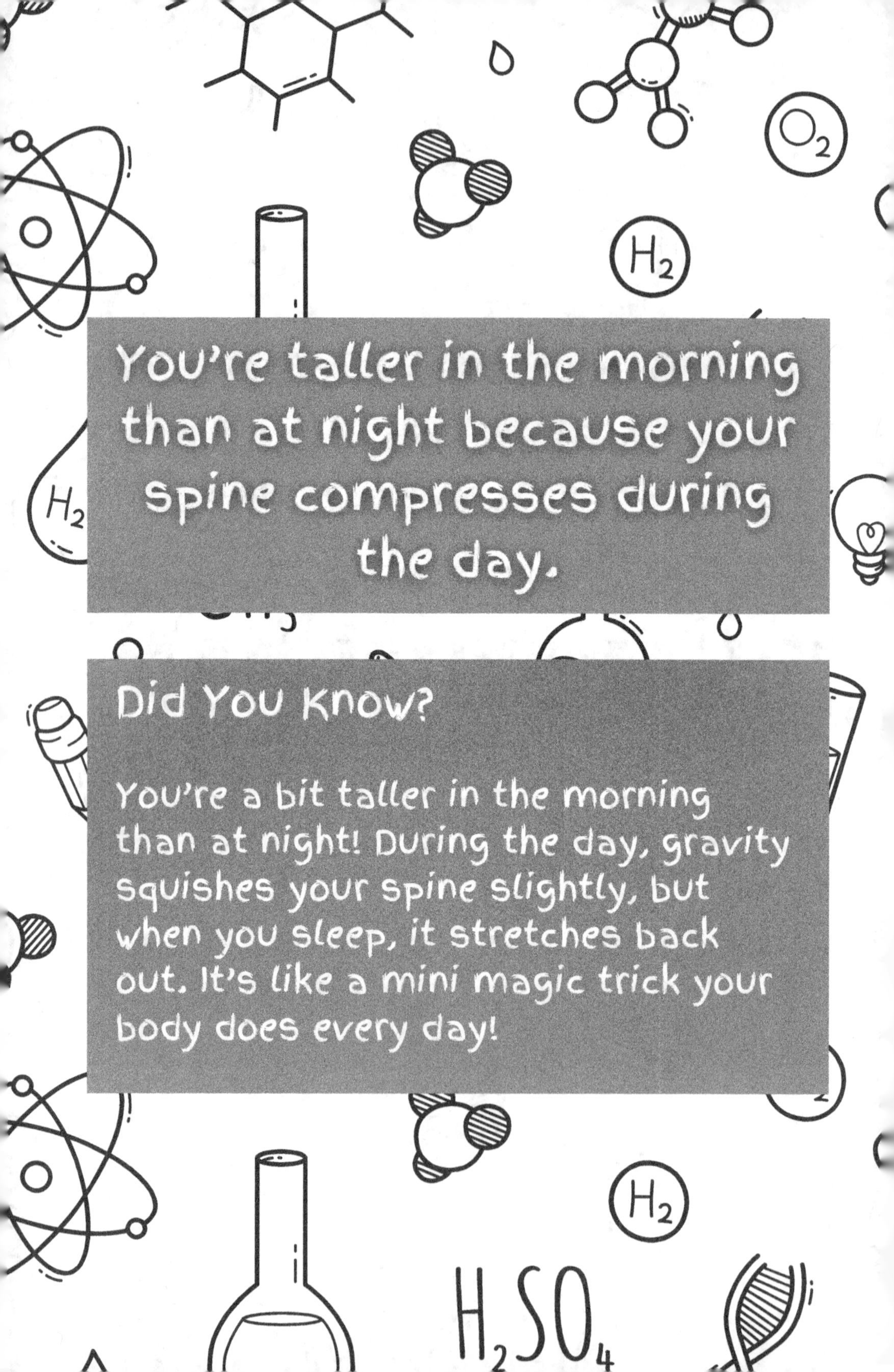
You're taller in the morning than at night because your spine compresses during the day.

Did You Know?

You're a bit taller in the morning than at night! During the day, gravity squishes your spine slightly, but when you sleep, it stretches back out. It's like a mini magic trick your body does every day!

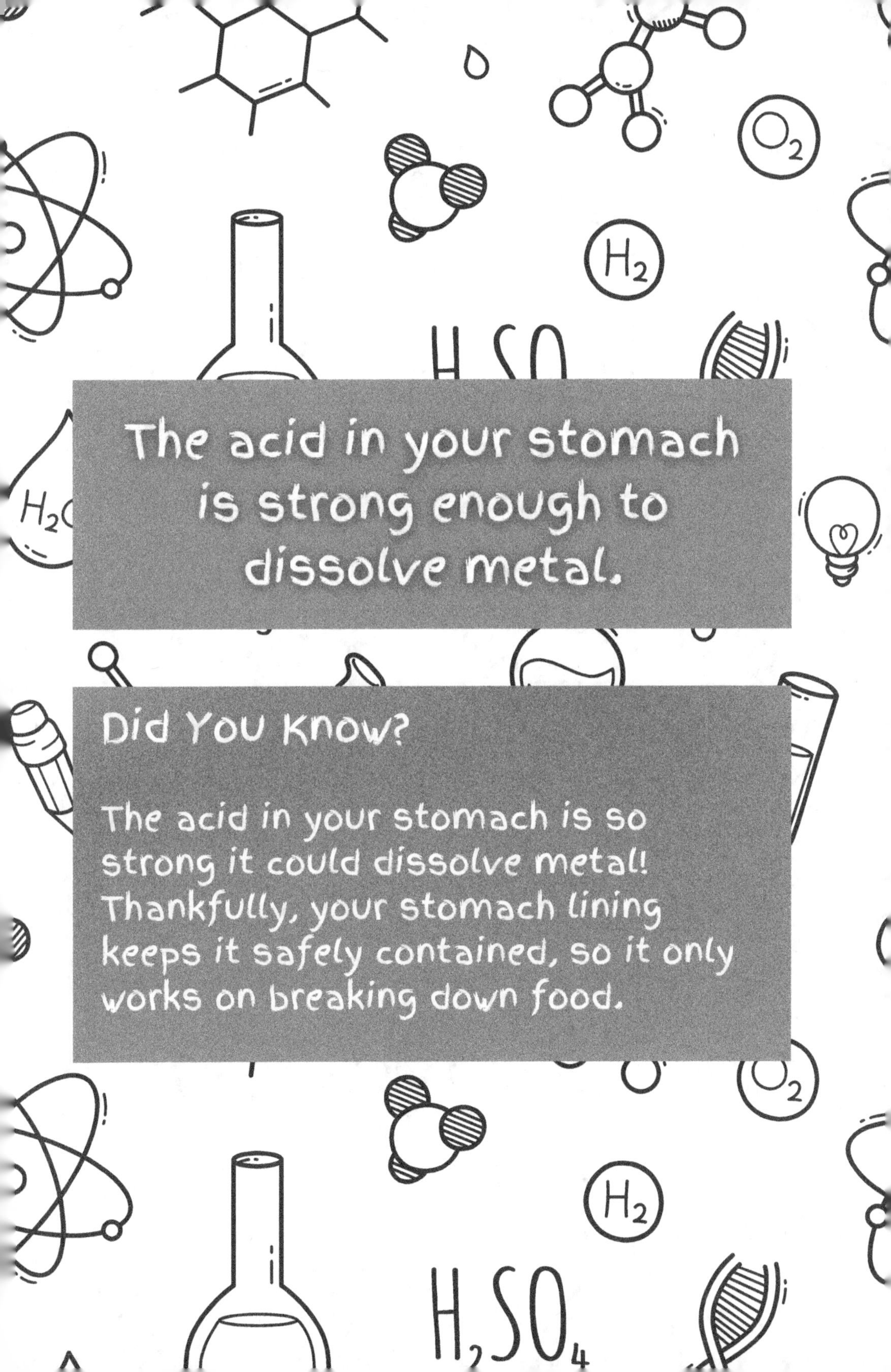
The acid in your stomach is strong enough to dissolve metal.

Did You Know?

The acid in your stomach is so strong it could dissolve metal! Thankfully, your stomach lining keeps it safely contained, so it only works on breaking down food.

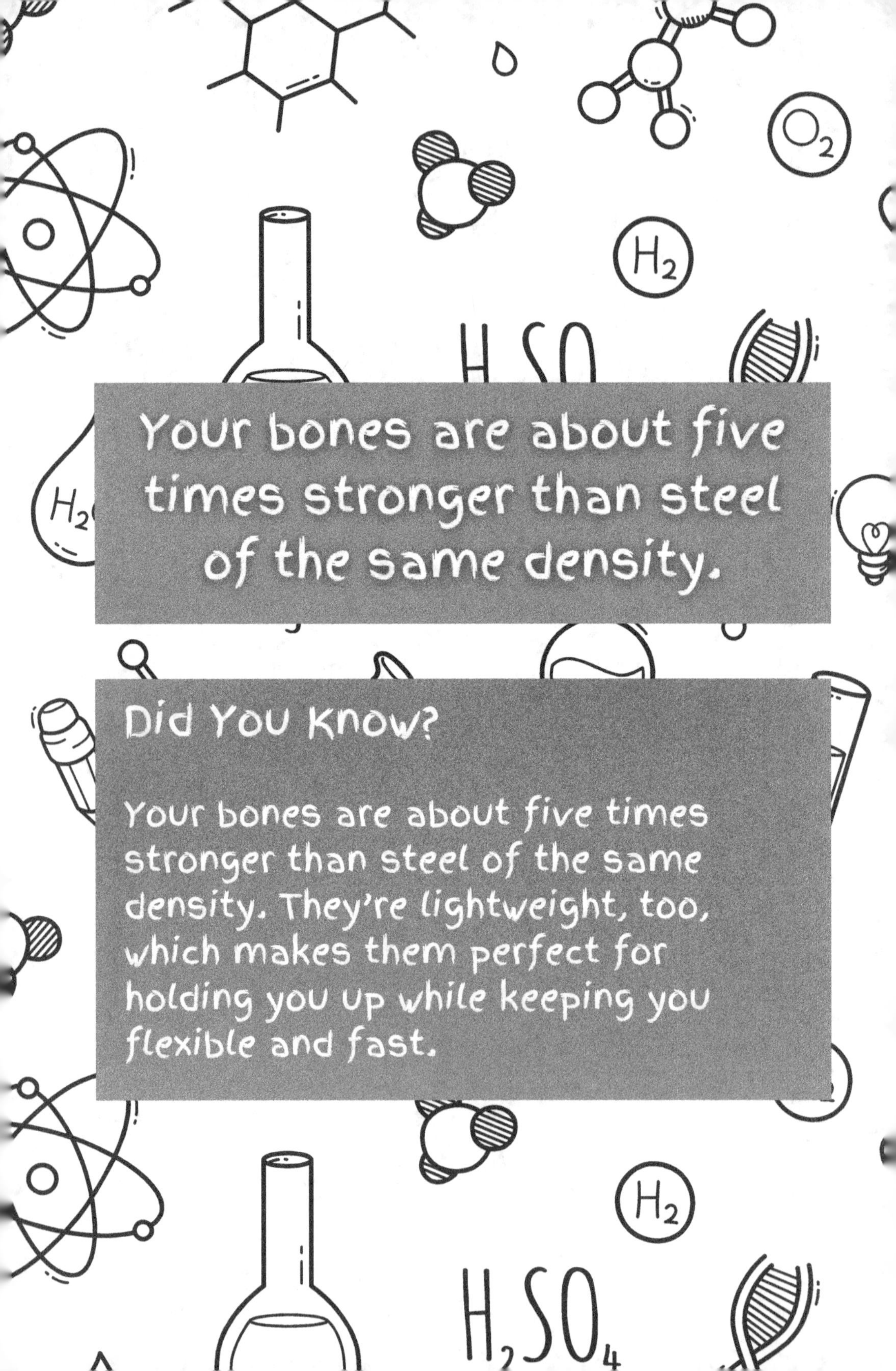

Your bones are about *five times stronger than steel* of the same density.

Did You Know?

Your bones are about *five times* stronger than steel of the same density. They're lightweight, too, which makes them perfect for holding you up while keeping you flexible and fast.

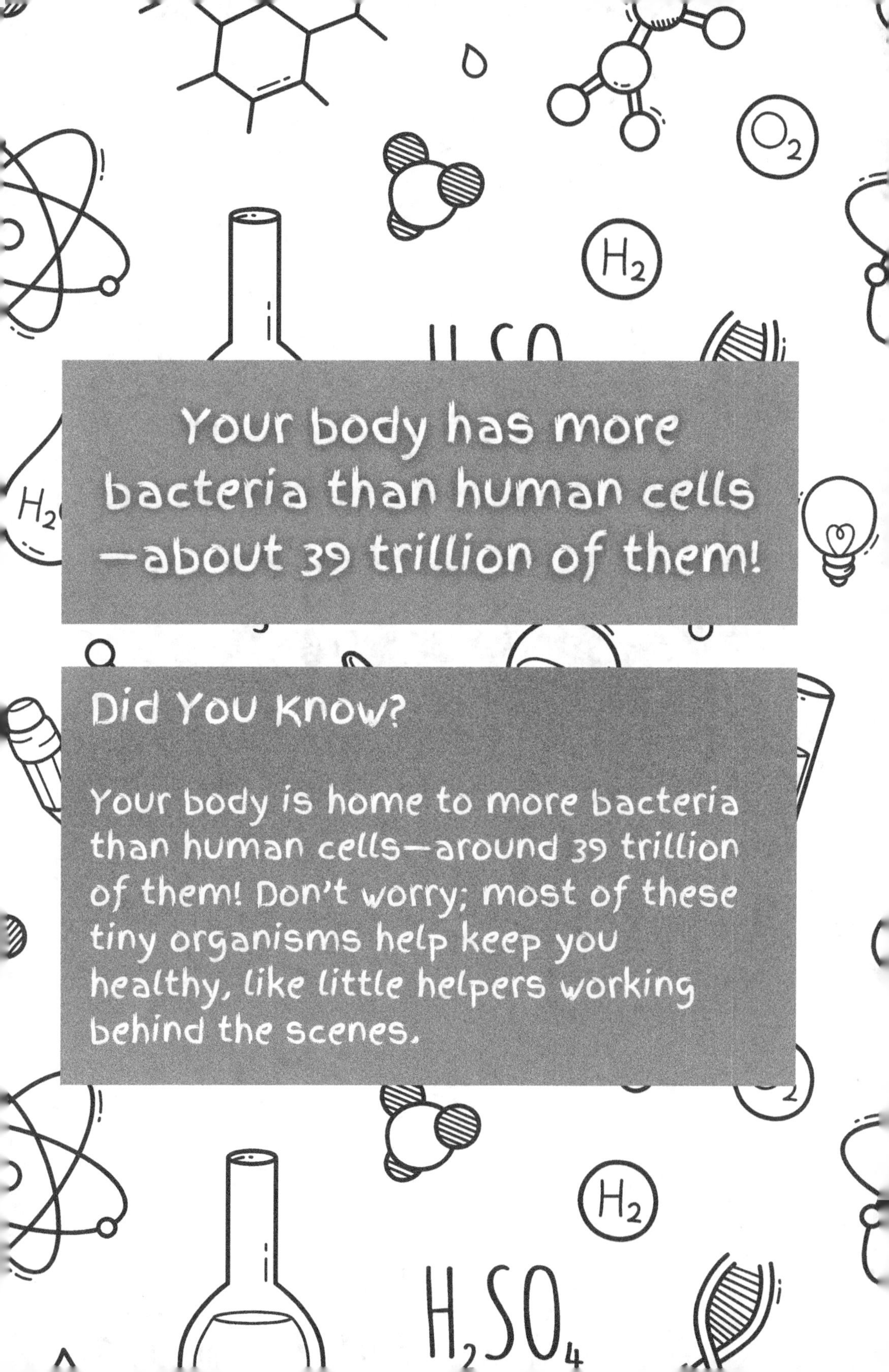

Your body has more bacteria than human cells—about 39 trillion of them!

Did You Know?

Your body is home to more bacteria than human cells—around 39 trillion of them! Don't worry; most of these tiny organisms help keep you healthy, like little helpers working behind the scenes.

The human nose can detect over 1 trillion different smells.

Did You Know?

Your nose is a super sniffer! It can detect over 1 trillion different smells, from cookies baking to fresh-cut grass. That's a whole lot of sniffing power!

Goosebumps are a leftover reflex from when humans had more body hair.

Did You Know?

Goosebumps happen when tiny muscles in your skin pull your hairs upright. Long ago, when humans had more body hair, this made us look bigger and scarier to predators. Now, it's just a cool leftover reflex!

Babies are born with about 300 bones, but adults only have 206 as some fuse together.

Did You Know?

Babies are born with about 300 bones, but as they grow, some of the bones fuse together. Adults end up with 206 bones, perfectly designed to support and protect them. It's like a puzzle that changes as you grow!

History

Cleopatra lived closer in time to the invention of the iphone than to the construction of the Great Pyramid of Giza

Did You Know?

Cleopatra lived closer in time to the invention of the iphone than to the building of the Great Pyramid of Giza! The pyramids were built around 4,500 years ago, but Cleopatra lived just 2,000 years ago. Isn't it wild to think about history like that?

In 1923, jockey Frank Hayes won a horse race despite dying during it.

Did You Know?

In 1923, jockey Frank Hayes won a horse race even though he passed away during the race! His horse, Sweet Kiss, kept running and crossed the finish line first, making it a very strange and unforgettable victory.

The shortest war in history lasted 38 minutes between Britain and Zanzibar in 1896.

Did You Know?

The shortest war in history lasted just 38 minutes! In 1896, Britain and Zanzibar went to war, and it was over almost as soon as it started. It's like the ultimate blink-and-you-miss-it battle.

During the Great Emu War in Australia, soldiers lost a battle against emus.

Did You Know?

In 1932, Australian soldiers tried to control emus, big flightless birds, in what became known as the Great Emu War. Guess what? The emus won! They were too fast and clever to be caught. Nature: 1, Humans: 0.

President John Adams and Thomas Jefferson both died on July 4, 1826 —America's 50th Independence Day.

Did You Know?

John Adams and Thomas Jefferson, two U.S. presidents, both died on July 4, 1826—exactly 50 years after the Declaration of Independence. It's a strange and historic coincidence!

King Tut's parents were siblings, which may explain his health problems.

Did You Know?

King Tut's parents were brother and sister, which might explain why he had so many health problems. Back then, royal families often married relatives to keep power in the family, but it wasn't great for their health.

The Eiffel Tower grows taller by about 6 inches in summer due to heat expansion.

Did You Know?

In summer, the Eiffel Tower grows taller by about 6 inches! When metal heats up, it expands, so the tower stretches a little before shrinking back in cooler weather. It's like the tower's seasonal stretch!

Medieval knights slept with their swords to stay ready for battle.

Did You Know?

Medieval knights were so prepared for battle that they slept with their swords by their side. If trouble came, they could leap into action right away. Talk about being ready 24/7!

Abraham Lincoln was a licensed bartender before becoming president.

Did You Know?

Before becoming president, Abraham Lincoln was a licensed bartender. He even co-owned a tavern! Who knew one of America's greatest leaders had experience serving drinks?

In ancient Rome, flamingo tongues were considered a delicacy.

Did You Know?

In ancient Rome, people considered flamingo tongues a fancy delicacy. It might sound odd to us, but back then, they were a luxury food for the rich. What unusual tastes they had!

Food

Honey never spoils

Did You Know?

Honey is like nature's time capsule—it never goes bad! Archaeologists have found jars of honey in ancient Egyptian tombs that are over 3,000 years old, and they're still safe to eat. Honey's low moisture and natural acids make it a forever food!

Ketchup was sold as medicine in the 1800s.

Did You Know?

In the 1800s, ketchup wasn't just a tasty topping—it was sold as medicine! People believed it could cure stomach problems. It wasn't until later that ketchup became the condiment we know and love today.

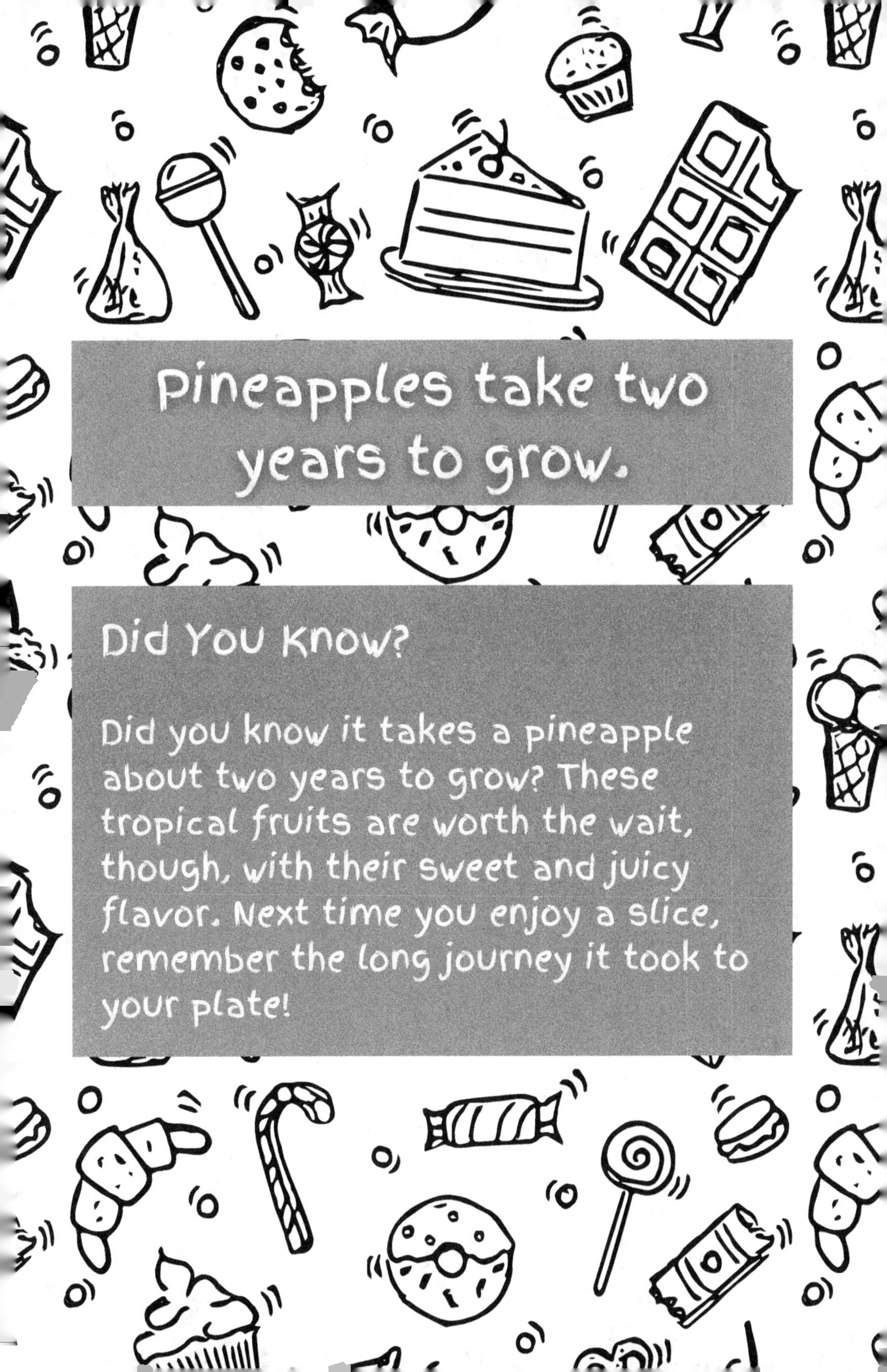

pineapples take two
years to grow.

Did You Know?

Did you know it takes a pineapple
about two years to grow? These
tropical fruits are worth the wait,
though, with their sweet and juicy
flavor. Next time you enjoy a slice,
remember the long journey it took to
your plate!

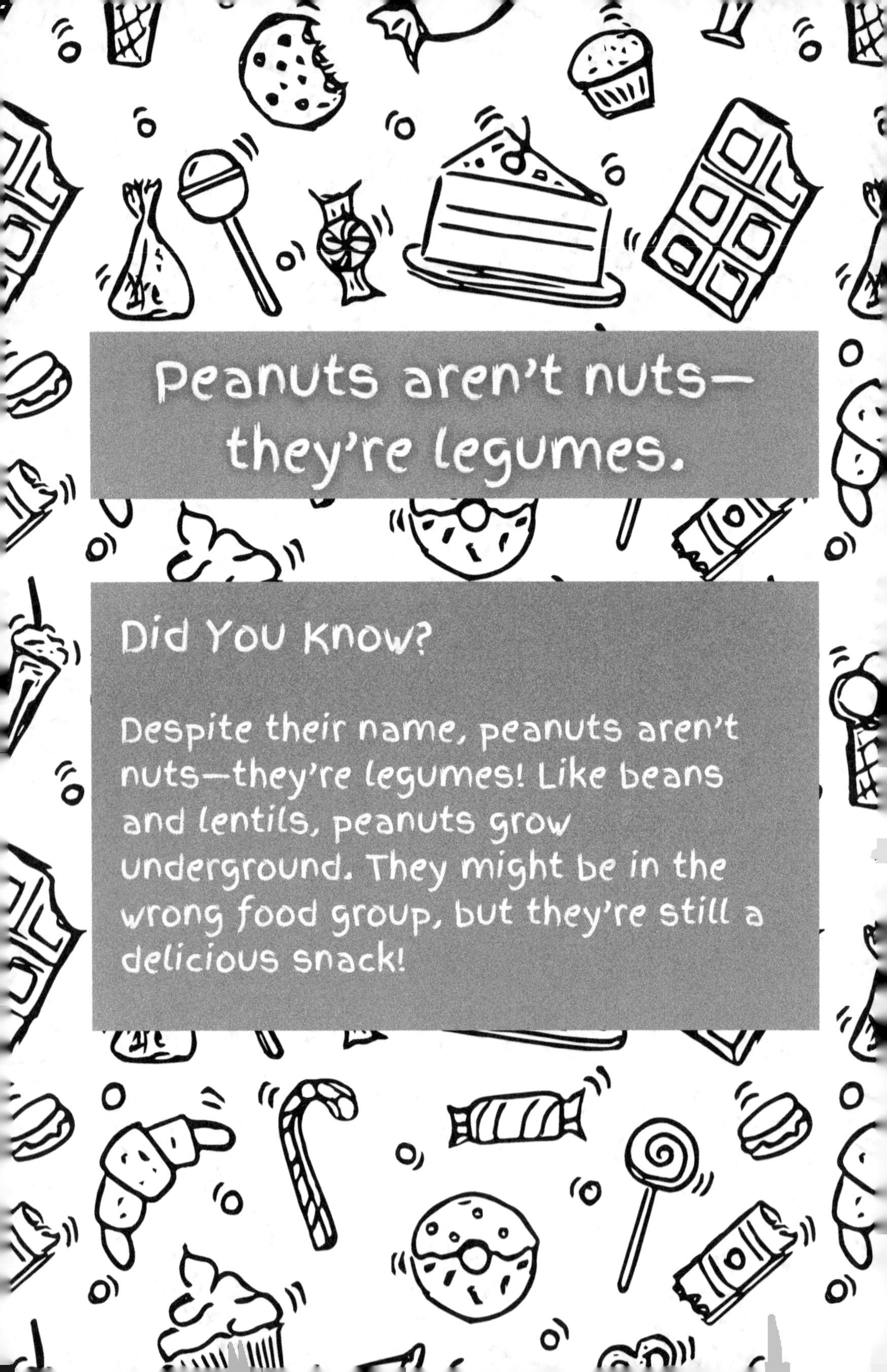

peanuts aren't nuts—
they're legumes.

Did You Know?

Despite their name, peanuts aren't nuts—they're legumes! Like beans and lentils, peanuts grow underground. They might be in the wrong food group, but they're still a delicious snack!

The world's most expensive coffee comes from beans that have been eaten and pooped out by a civet cat.

Did You Know?

The priciest coffee in the world is made from beans that have been eaten and pooped out by a civet cat. Called kopi luwak, these beans are collected, cleaned, and turned into a rich, unique brew. Coffee lovers say it's worth the odd process!

Carrots used to be purple before orange became the common color.

Did You Know?

Before the 1600s, most carrots were purple! The orange ones we know today were developed in the Netherlands to honor their royal family. Purple carrots are still around and just as tasty.

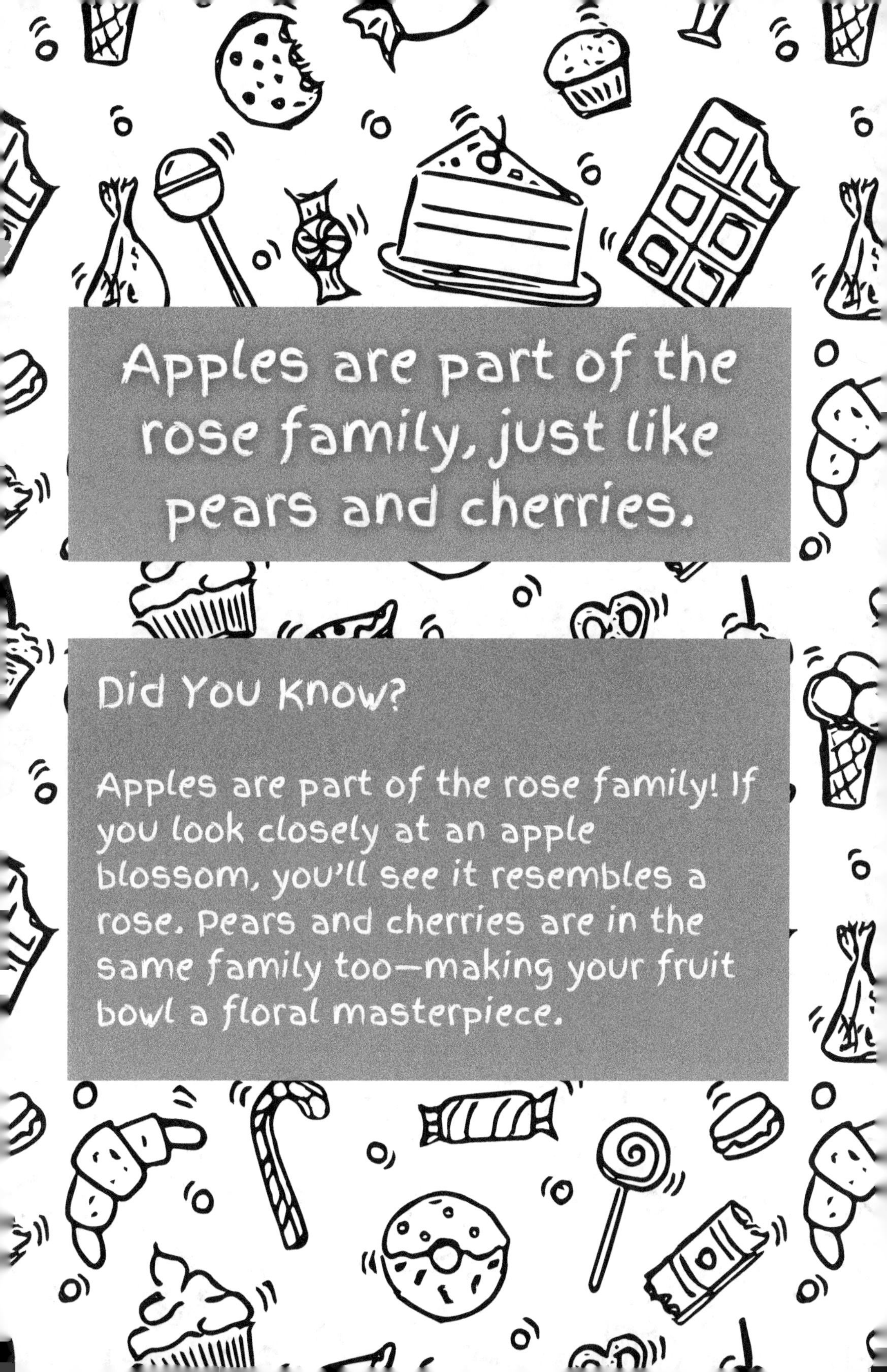

Apples are part of the rose family, just like pears and cherries.

Did You Know?

Apples are part of the rose family! If you look closely at an apple blossom, you'll see it resembles a rose. Pears and cherries are in the same family too—making your fruit bowl a floral masterpiece.

Hot dogs were once called "dachshund sausages."

Did You Know?

Hot dogs were originally called "dachshund sausages" because they looked like the long, skinny dogs. German immigrants brought them to America, where the name eventually changed—but the tasty treat stayed the same!

There's a fruit called a "miracle berry" that makes sour foods taste sweet.

Did You Know?

Honey is like nature's time capsule—it never goes bad! Archaeologists have found jars of honey in ancient Egyptian tombs that are over 3,000 years old, and they're still safe to eat. Honey's low moisture and natural acids make it a forever food!

watermelons were first
domesticated in Africa

Did You Know?

Honey is like nature's time capsule—
it never goes bad! Archaeologists
have found jars of honey in ancient
Egyptian tombs that are over 3,000
years old, and they're still safe to
eat. Honey's low moisture and
natural acids make it a forever food!

Guess
the
Fact

Can you figure out which of these statements is true? Only one is real give it your best guess!

- Honey can turn into a rock after 1,000 years.

- Hot dogs were originally called "dachshund sausages."

- Pineapples grow underground like potatoes.

Can you figure out which of these statements is true?

- Carrots were always orange and never any other color.

- Ketchup was once sold as medicine.

- Peanuts are considered a type of nut.

Can you figure out which of these statements is true?

- Frogs can freeze solid in winter and thaw out alive in spring.

- Alligators can climb trees.

- Birds don't have bones; they have cartilage instead.

Answer: Frogs can freeze solid in winter and thaw out alive in spring!

Can you figure out which of these statements is true?

• Venus spins backward compared to most planets.

• The Sun is made of solid rock.

• Jupiter has a smooth surface with no storms.

Answer: Venus spins backward compared to most planets!

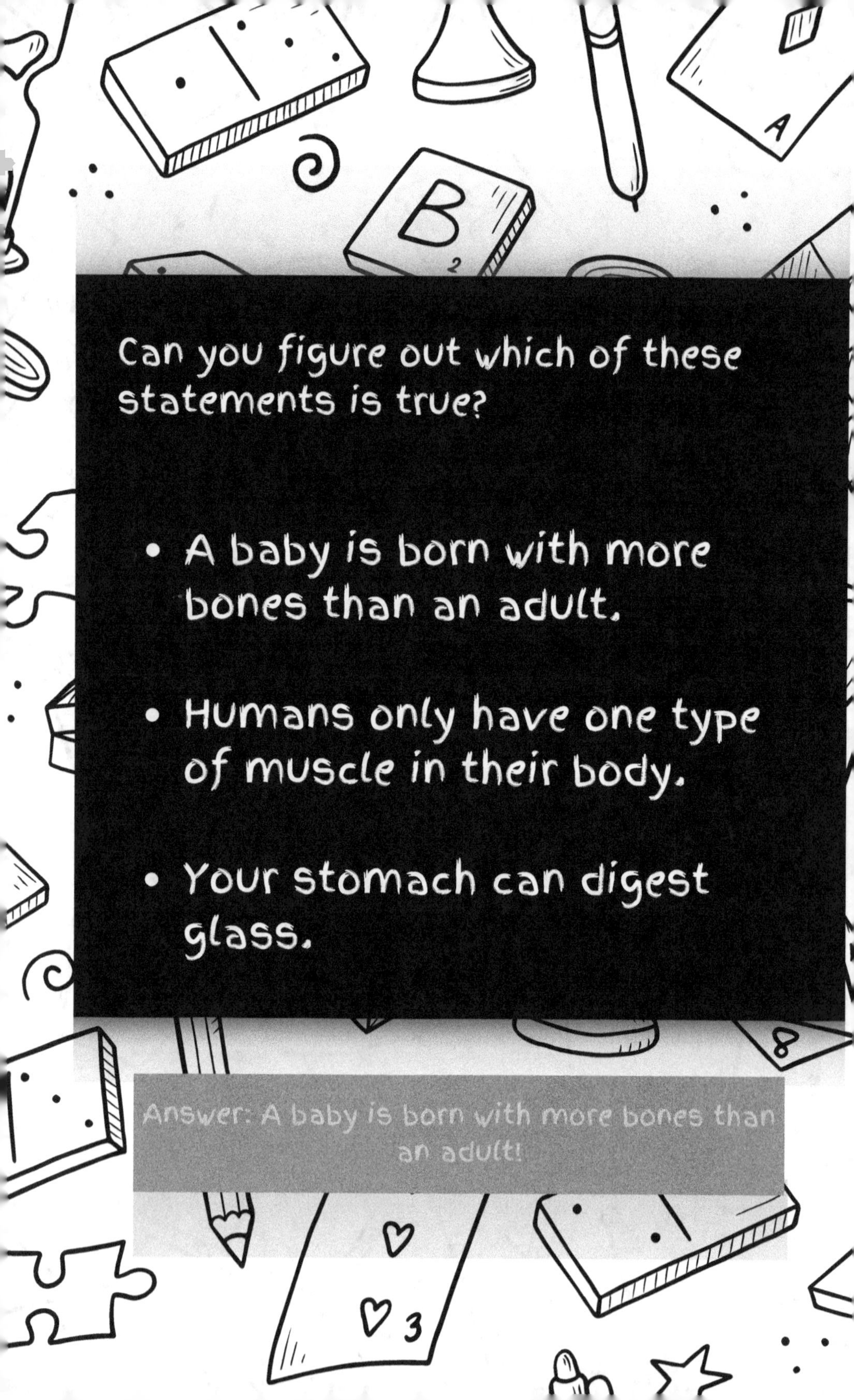

Can you figure out which of these statements is true?

- A baby is born with more bones than an adult.

- Humans only have one type of muscle in their body.

- Your stomach can digest glass.

Answer: A baby is born with more bones than an adult!

Can you figure out which of these statements is true?

- Sloths are faster than dolphins.

- Elephants can jump if they're running.

- A group of crows is called a murder.

Answer: A group of crows is called a murder!

Can you figure out which of these statements is true?

- Neutron stars are so dense that a teaspoon would weigh a billion tons.

- A day on Jupiter is longer than a year on Jupiter.

- Space smells like fresh flowers.

Answer: Neutron stars are so dense that a teaspoon would weigh a billion tons!

Can you figure out which of these statements is true?

• The Eiffel Tower shrinks in the summer due to heat.

• Honey can spoil if it's left out too long.

• Flamingos get their pink color from the food they eat.

Answer: Flamingos get their pink color from the food they eat!

Can you figure out which of these statements is true?

- Watermelons were first grown for their sweetness.

- Apples are part of the rose family.

- pineapples grow on trees.

Can you figure out which of these statements is true?

• There's a fruit that makes sour foods taste sweet.

• Bananas grow upside down underground.

• Strawberries are true berries.

Answer: There's a fruit that makes sour foods taste sweet! (It's called the "miracle berry.")

Solve
the
maze

START
Maze 1
FINISH

START
Maze 2
FINISH
3
3

START
Maze 3
FINISH

START
Maze 4
FINISH

START
Maze 5
FINISH

Thank You for Reading!
"Thank you for exploring this fun-filled book of facts, puzzles, and challenges! I hope you learned something new, laughed a little, and enjoyed the journey. Stay curious, keep exploring, and never stop having fun!"

Stay Curious!
"Curiosity is the key to discovering the world around you. Keep asking questions, exploring new ideas, and making every day an adventure!"